Live Your Life, On Purpose

Welcome to the Life on Purpose Workbook

This book is a compilation of many things . . . .

My experience: I used to live on autopilot and felt I was like a victim of my life.

I had a hard journey early in motherhood. I was anxious, exhausted and restless. My marriage was struggling, my health, my home, and my relationships were slipping.

I learned about minimalism and started decluttering my home. I was face to face with a life full of so much 'stuff'. I had never thought to question what should get to stay and what I needed to let go of.

As I let go of stuff I saw so many ways I was complacent in my life and my thinking. I lived so many years on autopilot, just reacting to life.

I did all the 'safe' things. I went to college, got the secure job, married, bought the house and the vehicles. But this was all just chasing the definition of success set out in the culture before me. I didn't question that I could quit a job I hate and try something different. I didn't question that I could live with a lot less than I what I thought I needed. I didn't let difficulties grow me, I made them mean I was failing. I needed a new definition of what a successful life looked like.

I never considered that I was in charge. I didn't take responsibility for building up a life I wanted. I didn't even really think about the life I wanted. I hadn't listened to myself. I hadn't held myself accountable.

As I started to learn about 'intentional living' my husband and I started planning goals and setting vision for our family.

I worked on changing my habits and doing the things that really made me feel like I was the mom/wife/friend/woman I wanted to be.

Life began to feel manageable, and then fun, and then freeing!

Year on Purpose Workbook: This workbook is the super expanded version of the free workbook on the website that many of my readers have downloaded and loved. It has helped me in planning my year and has helped the many people who have used it.

Whole Life Vision: This workbook includes exercises I use in my Life Coaching Program. Particularly, the Whole Life Vision, which involves assessing the various areas of your life, setting vision for them and making changes to reach that vision.

Life Coaching: I don't just life coach my clients, I coach myself. Everyday we are faced with our thought patterns and limiting mindsets. We don't realize they are there until we stop and seek them out. We don't realize how they hinder us until we can see how these thoughts affect our feelings and, therefore, our actions. In this book I bring in some foundational teachings I have learned and use in life coaching myself and my clients.

>> MAKE SURE to sign up for the bonus tips, videos and worksheets at www.simpleonpurpose.ca/workbook-bonuses

the goal of this workbook

When you live your life on purpose you will feel in control, purposeful and productive. I wrote this book because I needed it when I was learning how to live my life on purpose.

The whole premise of this book is to evaluate the ways we live on auto-pilot and plan out how we want to take over control and direction of our one precious life.

Almost everything we do is on auto-pilot. How we think, how we react, the things we put off, the stories we tell ourselves. This book offers a space to pause and assess what IS happening on your life.

Further to that, this book allows you space to listen closer to yourself and what you do want. This is important because when you take the time to determine what success looks like for you — it becomes fulfilling and authentic to you.

Finally, this book will wrap up with ways to put it all into action.

The goal of this book is to give you the jump start on living YOUR life ON PURPOSE.

This book will help you to:
- Pay attention to yourself and examine what you truly want in your life
- See areas of your life that need your attention this year
- Form a vision for your life that is exciting and inspiring
- Broaden your thinking about your life
- Identify your core values
- Set some goals you never had before
- Lay everything out in an organized way that feels approachable

Table of Contents

The Whole Life Vision   7

Identify Your Personal Values   11

Terms To Remember   14

Set Your Whole Life Vision   15

Home   17

Family   22

Love/Marriage   27

Health   32

Friendships/Community   37

Work   42

Outer Expression   47

Inner Expression   52

Finances   57

Simplify   62

Plan Your Life on Purpose   65

Powerful Habits   75

Live It Out   81

Being Mindful   84

Monthly Reflection   85

Staying on Track   88

The Whole Life Vision

We start with setting a vision for our life, and identifying our core values.

vision before goals

A vision is the bigger picture, a hope for the future. It is the destination and goals are how we get there.

We might want to jump in and set some goals, but we need to know WHERE we are going before we set the steps to get there. Our goals help us move in the direction of our vision. They support the vision.

When we set a goal without a vision, our goal might be set for the wrong reasons. Or it might not actually serve us in our bigger vision. It might also be a way of 'striving' for status or comfort.

Goals can also be a hindrance when they feel overwhelming. They need to be rooted in the vision to feel necessary and inspiring.

For instance, if my 'goal' is to declutter my basement, that is overwhelming and I'm not excited to get started. I'll probably be looking for ways to put it off. I will grumble when it is time to do the work.

However, if I have a *vision* of turning my basement into a bright, clear space that my kids can play and create in — then this is inspiring and motivating. I am more likely to get the goal done, because it is serving a bigger purpose and passion, my vision.

what is a vision?

In this workbook, vision is defined as what you *want*, what you crave for areas of your life.

It can be described with smell, sight, and sound. I encourage you to focus on how it *feels* to yourself and those around you.

When you are setting your vision make sure you filter out the voice of others. Listen closely to yourself and *what you want* versus what you think you *should* want (which is from the expectation of others).

why is it important?

When we set out a vision we get to choose the life we build up, rather than just live on auto-pilot, reacting to whatever comes our way, and feeling let down that our life isn't what we want it to be.

Setting a vision for our life will be more motivating than setting goals. Because our vision has positive feelings attached to it (eg. with my basement vision it makes me *feel* free, creative, open).

Focussing on these feelings we want in our lives is important because we are most motivated by feelings. How often do we rely on our feelings to get us to do something? Each time we find ourselves saying "I don't feel like it" it is happening.

Or we might not realize we do this, because we might layer on a bunch of 'logic' about *why* we don't feel like it (it's a bad time, this other thing needs to be done, etc.). We make these other things the reason we don't do 'the thing' — but the reality is we don't do many things in our day because we simply don't feel like it.

It is unfortunate we let our feelings be our main motivational tool but we can also harness this situation to serve us. We can focus on the positive feelings our vision will give us, and turn to those as our motivation.

living in line with our values

Our vision paints a big picture and in this picture we will see our values shining through.

Our values are those qualities that we believe are vital to how we live our life. We use them to guide our decisions because we identify with them deeply. Our personal values are a compass for the life we want to live.

On a daily basis we have opportunities to live in line with our values. When we don't, we can feel this uncomfortable tension. We aren't living a life that is reflective of our values, of our core identity, and that feels inauthentic and frustrating.

For example, in parenting I might have the value of peace. So when I am disciplining my kids, or on an outing with them - I might be the opposite of peaceful. I will feel gross about parenting, unsure about the exact reasons why, and this tension seeps into other areas of my life.

I need to find ways to act out my value of peace in my parenting.

This tension can be a source of anxiety for many people and we might not realize it is happening — we just realize that things feel off. Often, this tension can accumulate and we end feeling frazzled with the day, and confused about why our life doesn't 'feel right'.

When we live out our values, on a daily basis *and* on a big life-scale, we will feel more authentic, peaceful and productive.

knowing our personal values

A lot of us live with this tension of not living according to our values simply because we haven't taken the time to identify our vision and values. This tension, this anxiety, can make us feel like something is wrong with us, or our relationships, or our life.

We aren't broken. We have just been on autopilot. We haven't been paying attention to ourselves or what we want or how we want to get it.

This is why it is so helpful to sit down and map out our vision and identify our values, it gives us a direction for our days and decisions. When we live in line with our values we feel more at peace and more proactive.

"You need to find a way to live your life that it doesn't make a mockery of your values"

- Bill Ayers

Identify Your Personal Values

It is important to take the time to decide which values are most *important to you* in how you live during this season of your life.

Look at the list of values on the next page and circle the ones that resonate with you.

Remember, there are no wrong answers. This is a time for you to listen to yourself and to get back in touch with those qualities and ways of being in the world that are a part of who you are.

> "When your values are clear to you, making decisions becomes easier"
>
> - Roy Disney

personal values list

Review this list and circle ones that are important to you at this stage of your life. Circle as many as you like. Feel free to add more.

Achievement	Action	Accuracy	Adaptability
Adventure	Affection	Balance	Beauty
Boldness	Bravery	Calmness	Challenge
Collaboration	Comfort	Community	Competence
Connection	Contentment	Creativity	Curiosity
Dedication	Dependability	Determination	Discipline
Discovery	Education	Efficiency	Empathy
Environment	Equality	Faith	Family
Fearless	Flexibility	Focus	Freedom
Frugality	Generosity	Gratitude	Greatness
Growth	Hardworking	Helpfulness	Honesty
Hope	Humility	Humour	Imagination
Impact	Independence	Individuality	Innovation
Insight	Inspiration	Integrity	Inviting
Intentional	Joyful	Justice	Kindness
Knowledge	Leadership	Lively	Logical
Mastery	Mellow	Mindfulness	Moderation
Modesty	Openness	Optimism	Order
Originality	Partnership	Passion	Patience

Peace	Performance	Playfulness	Potential
Preservation	Privacy	Productivity	Professionalism
Profitable	Recognition	Recreation	Relational
Reliability	Resourcefulness	Respect	Responsibility
Rest	Results	Risk	Sacrifice
Safety	Security	Selflessness	Service
Simplicity	Skillfulness	Spirituality	Spontaneity
Stability	Status	Strength	Success
Support			

1. Now, go through that values list again. Even though a value is on your list, it is still worth questioning each one.

    Look over it and challenge each one.
    - Is this a value you think you 'should' have?
    - Is it one you were raised with but never really wanted?
    - Is this value a temporary solution or a permanent part of your vision?
    - Does this value energize you or exhaust you?

2. Edit your values list accordingly.

3. Highlight your top 5 values.

Use this list for reference as you work through the whole life vision.

Terms To Remember

VISION

The hope you have for your future. The vision is how it feels and how it looks to you. It is your dream, your destination.

e.g. I have a vision for my finances to be sustainably earned with a job that allows me freedom, and my money is spent and saved wisely.

VALUES

The ideals that you want to live your life according to. The priorities for how the work gets done, or how you want to show up.

e.g. frugality, self-employment, work-life balance

GOALS

A project/task/accomplishment that you want to reach. It must be specific and measurable.

e.g. I want to save up three months income incase of emergency

ACTION STEPS

The actions I can take to reach my goal

e.g. meet with a financial planner, make a budget, set up a savings account, set up automated deposits

HABITS

A practice that you want to be part of your regular routine.

e.g. I routinely track my spending to see where my money is going and to stick to a budget

Set Your Whole Life Vision

We use this whole life approach because when we set vision we need to address all the areas of our life, individually, because they all support one another. Finding passion and purpose in one area of our life can leak over to all the other areas. Likewise, feeling incomplete or hindered in one area can ripple into other areas of our life. Every part counts.

There are nine categories to cover:

We are not just one of these parts, we are a sum of them. They all matter to the fullness of our life.

As you go through each category, set out the vision you have for it. You can use lists, or paragraphs, whatever style you like. You may answer any of the prompts you like or just freestyle it. You determine the timeframe you are setting the vision for. I recommend setting it for the next 2-5 years.

the art of good questions

"The quality of your life is directly related to the quality of questions you ask yourself"

This workbook is designed in a way that reflects how a life coach would work with a client — by asking effective questions to help you unearth the root answer.

The art of quality questioning can help us uncover our motivations, our mindsets, our vision, and our blind spots. This is the work a life coach does — asking the good questions to help you see yourself and your life more clearly, then setting the next steps to get to where you want to be.

By focussing on questions that challenge us we can grow in self awareness. By focussing on 'the how' we become more solution minded.

I encourage you to spend time with the questions in this workbook. Sit with them, listen closely to yourself. Don't judge your answers as right or wrong, just let them tell you what is happening for you on a deeper level.

Home

Questions to help you form your vision for your home:

How do I want to feel in my home?

What do I want my home to be for my family?

How do I want others to feel in my home?

What makes me feel like I am running my home well?

What things do I want my home to be used for?

What values are important in how my home feels?

- *Use this space to get all your thoughts out on what your vision is for this area of your life. This space is for brainstorming, first thoughts and rough notes. The questions above are to help you think about different aspects of a vision — answer whichever ones you wish.*

evaluate

Home

What is your LEVEL OF CONTENTMENT in this area of your life? On a scale of 1-10, rate how content you are in this area of your life, as it is now. (1 being completely discontent, 10 being completely content).

1   2   3   4   5   6   7   8   9   1 0

As life currently is, what is working well in this area?

As life currently is, what is not working in this area?

What am I responsible for when it comes to what isn't working well?

plan

What are ways I can own my responsibility and make positive changes?

When it comes to this area of my life, I want to do more:

When it comes to this area of my life, I want to do less:

What are things/rooms/areas in my home that bring me stress/need to be changed?

Do I have any specific goals (1 year, 5 year, 10 year) for my home?

vision

Taking your notes from above, sum up (in a few sentences) the overall vision you have for this area of life:

values

Top three values for my home life:

    1

    2

    3

success

In the past, how have I defined success in this area?

Moving forward, how do I want to define success in this area?

This list on this page is a for you to put all your ideas on ways you could live out your vision. List all the ideas you can think of.

Remember, you don't have to do everything listed here, and don't have to do it all this year. Use this space to get all your ideas out onto paper then highlight your favourites.

And if you can't think of much, just write down a possible next step you could make — something you think would be interesting or useful to try/do/learn.

Brainstorm on ways to achieve my vision:

habits/routines

goals/projects

Home

Family

What kind of culture do I want my family to have?

What values do I want my kids to have?

What are things I want my kids to do/learn?

How do I want to show up as a parent?

What values are important to me in how I parent?

What are my parenting strengths that I can draw from?

evaluate

Family

On a scale of 1-10, rate how content you are in this area of your life, as it is now.

1   2   3   4   5   6   7   8   9   10

As life currently is, what is working well in this area?

As life currently is, what is not working well in this area?

What am I responsible for when it comes to what isn't working well?

plan

What are ways I can own my responsibility and make positive changes?

In my family life, I want to do more:

In my family life, I want to do less:

Do I have any specific goals (1 year, 5 year, 10 year) for myself in this area?

List each of your kids/immediate family members and note any ways you want to pour into them, guide them, and appreciate them in this coming year.

vision

Taking your notes from above, sum up (in a few sentences) the overall vision you have for this area of life:

values

Top three values for my family life

1

2

3

success

In the past, how have I defined success in this area?

Moving forward, how do I want to define success in this area?

Brainstorm on ways to achieve my vision:

family habits/traditions	family bucket list

Love/Marriage

(I use the term marriage in the questions but this section is for any love relationship)

What qualities do I want my marriage to have?

What do I want my marriage to feel like?

How do I want to show up in my marriage?

What values are important to me in how I act in my marriage?

What do I love most about my marriage and how can I pour into that?

evaluate

On a scale of 1-10, rate how content you are in this area of your life, as it is now.

1   2   3   4   5   6   7   8   9   10

As life currently is, what is working well in this area?

As life currently is, what is not working in this area?

What am I responsible for when it comes to what isn't working well?

plan

What are ways I can own my responsibility and make positive changes?

In my love relationship want to do more:

In my love relationship I want to do less:

What things am I most grateful for in my partner?

Do I have any specific goals (1 year, 5 year, 10 year) for myself in this area?

vision

Taking your notes from above, sum up (in a few sentences) the overall vision you have for this area of life:

values

Top three values for my marriage

    1

    2

    3

success

In the past, how have I defined success in this area?

Moving forward, how do I want to define success in this area?

Brainstorm on ways to achieve my vision:

marriage habits	marriage bucket list

Health

(pertaining to your physical health, food, sleep, fitness, mental health)

What does healthy living look like to me?

Why is health important to me?

How do I feel when I am taking good care of myself?

What values are important in how I approach my health?

What has to happen for me to be healthy?

Where areas of healthy living are of most interest to me?

evaluate

On a scale of 1-10, rate how content you are in this area of your life, as it is now.

1   2   3   4   5   6   7   8   9   1 0

As life currently is, what is working well in this area?

As life currently is, what is not working in this area?

What am I responsible for when it comes to what isn't working well?

plan

What are ways I can own my responsibility and make positive changes?

For my health, I want to do more:

For my health, I want to do less:

Do I have any specific goals (1 year, 5 year, 10 year) for myself in this area?

vision

Taking your notes from above, sum up (in a few sentences) the overall vision you have for this area of life:

Health

values

Top three values for my health

    1

    2

    3

success

In the past, how have I defined success in this area?

Moving forward, how do I want to define success in this area?

Brainstorm on ways to achieve my vision:

health habits/routines	health goals

Friendships/Community

What kind of friend do I want to be?

What types of friendships do I want to pour into?

How do I want to nurture/grow my friendships this year?

When friendship seems intimidating or difficult, what do I need to remember to be the type of friend I want to be?

What areas in my community do I want to pour into?

What role do I want to play in my community/neighbourhood?

What values are important for how I show up as a friend?

evaluate

On a scale of 1-10, rate how content you are in this area of your life, as it is now.

Friendships

1   2   3   4   5   6   7   8   9   1 0

As life currently is, what is working well in this area?

As life currently is, what is not working in this area?

What am I responsible for when it comes to what isn't working well?

plan

What are ways I can own my responsibility and make positive changes?

Friendships

When it comes to friendships, I want to do more:

When it comes to friendships, I want to do less:

Who are people/groups that I want to be more invested in this coming year?

Do I have any specific goals (1 year, 5 year, 10 year) for myself in this area?

Friendships

vision

Taking your notes from above, sum up (in a few sentences) the overall vision you have for this area of life:

values

Top three values for my friendships

1

2

3

success

In the past, how have I defined success in this area?

Moving forward, how do I want to define success in this area?

Brainstorm on ways to achieve my vision:

friendship habits/rituals	friendship bucket list

Work

(paid or volunteer)

What work do I find fulfilling?

How does work fit into this season of my life?

How do I define professional success?

What values are part of how I approach work?

How do I want to show up at work and act out my values?

What qualities are important to me in how I approach my work?

What is the next interesting thing I could pursue in my work?

evaluate

On a scale of 1-10, rate how content you are in this area of
your life, as it is now.

1   2   3   4   5   6   7   8   9   10

As life currently is, what is working well in this area?

As life currently is, what is not working in this area?

What am I responsible for when it comes to what isn't working well?

plan

What are ways I can own my responsibility and make positive changes?

When it comes to work, I want to do more:

When it comes to work, I want to do less:

What ways can develop my professional skills in this coming year?

Do I have any specific goals (1 year, 5 year, 10 year) for myself in this area?

vision

Taking your notes from above, sum up (in a few sentences) the overall vision you have for this area of life:

values

Top three values for my work life

     1

     2

     3

success

In the past, how have I defined success in this area?

Moving forward, how do I want to define success in this area?

Brainstorm on ways to achieve my vision:

work habits/routines	goals/projects

Outer Expression

(hobbies, creativity, style, recreation, etc.)

What makes me feel creative/inspired/alive?

What hobbies/activities do I hope will always be part of my life?

What are the ways I like to express myself?

What are some things I say I want to try and haven't yet?

What are things I loved doing as a kid and want to try again?

What spaces make me feel creative/inspired/alive?

What activities and hobbies might I do if I was alone?

evaluate

On a scale of 1-10, rate how content you are in this area of your life, as it is now.

1   2   3   4   5   6   7   8   9   10

As life currently is, what is working well in this area?

As life currently is, what is not working in this area?

What am I responsible for when it comes to what isn't working well?

plan

What are ways I can own my responsibility and make positive changes?

I want to do more:

I want to do less:

Do I have any specific goals (1 year, 5 year, 10 year) for myself in this area?

vision

Taking your notes from above, sum up (in a few sentences)
the overall vision you have for this area of life:

values

Top three values for my outer expression

     1

     2

     3

success

In the past, how have I defined success in this area?

Moving forward, how do I want to define success in this area?

Brainstorm on ways to achieve my vision:

habits/routines	goals/projects

Inner Expression

(personal growth, spirituality, emotional life, learning, self-development, higher meaning, etc.)

How do I want to grow emotionally? Spiritually?

What inner expression practices do I want to be a part of my daily life?

What areas do I want to grow in as a leader?

What values motivate me to grow as a person?

What do I want to learn more about?

What makes me feel like I am living a meaningful life?

What do I feel I am called to in my life?

What does personal growth look like for me in this area?

evaluate

On a scale of 1-10, rate how content you are in this area of your life, as it is now.

1   2   3   4   5   6   7   8   9   1 0

As life currently is, what is working well in this area?

As life currently is, what is not working in this area?

What am I responsible for when it comes to what isn't working well?

plan

What are ways I can own my responsibility and make positive changes?

When it comes to this area of my life, I want to do more:

When it comes to this areas of my life, I want to do less:

What is something specific I want to learn and grow in this coming year?

How can I grow in self-awareness this coming year?

Do I have any specific goals (1 year, 5 year, 10 year) for myself in this area?

vision

Taking your notes from above, sum up (in a few sentences) the overall vision you have for this area of life:

values

Top three values for my inner expression

1

2

3

success

In the past, how have I defined success in this area?

Moving forward, how do I want to define success in this area?

Brainstorm on ways to achieve my vision:

habits/routines	goals/projects

Finances

What values do I want to use in how I approach my finances?

What role do I want finances to play in my day to day life?

What financial goals and habits are important to me?

How do I want to earn my income?

What lifestyle is important to me and how do my finances support that?

What are my core beliefs around how money should be handled?

What things are a priority for me in where my money goes? (What things/ activities do you want your money to be spent on?)

evaluate

On a scale of 1-10, rate how content you are in this area of your life, as it is now.

1   2   3   4   5   6   7   8   9   10

As life currently is, what is working well in this area?

As life currently is, what is not working well in this area?

What am I responsible for when it comes to what isn't working well?

plan

What are ways I can own my responsibility and make positive changes?

Finances

When it comes to finances, I want to do more:

When it comes to finances, I want to do less:

What major expenses are coming up that I need to prepare for?

What things are priority for me to spend money on?

What things are not a priority for me to spend money on?

Do I have any specific goals (1 year, 5 year, 10 year) for myself in this area?

vision

Taking your notes from above, sum up (in a few sentences) the overall vision you have for this area of life:

values

Top three values for my finances

1

2

3

success

In the past, how have I defined success in this area?

Moving forward, how do I want to define success in this area?

Brainstorm on ways to achieve my vision:

financial habits	financial goals

Simplify

We can set vision and goals, but if we don't stop and clear the clutter we will just be steamrolling through our existing life. Steamrolling our existing life is a battle that will exhaust our resources.

Let's clear some space for new habits and goals to happen.

start with self awareness

→ *A great self-awareness tool I am always sharing is called the Enneagram. This tool shows you your stress behaviours and your core fears and motives. It is very eye-opening.*

All of our mindsets and habits have built up this life as it is. So take a moment to reflect on it. Consider what points have come up for you in the vision setting exercise and the season of life you are in.

>> What has been motivating me? What have I been trying to avoid, or trying to chase?

>> How do I act when I am under stress?

>> How do I act when I feel secure?

set a new direction

>> What do I want to be motivated by?

>> How do I want to act when I am under stress?

>> What are healthy ways that help me lower my stress?

>> How do I want to show up in my daily life?

keep the best, let go of the rest

Look at different areas of your life that could use a decluttering. If you go through the process to keep the 'best' and let go of the rest, how would that look to declutter in the following areas?

>> My time

>> My home

>> My online life

>> My relationships

>> My work

>> My hobbies

>> My thoughts

>> My spending

Plan Your Life on Purpose

For some of us the brainstorming and listening to ourselves is the hard part. For others (me included) DOING the thing is what is hard.

All of this work won't really make a change in our lives, unless we TAKE ACTION.

"Knowledge is of no use unless you put it into practice"

- **Anton Chekhov**

Let's take what you have learned about yourself and what you want, and put it into practice. I'm going to take you through the steps of putting your life vision into action. You have already done steps 1-4. Here is how to move forward in the year(s) to come.

action steps for the whole life vision

1. Set your values and vision
2. Set goals/projects and habits you want to pursue
3. Reflect on how you might hold yourself back
4. Clear the slate to start fresh
5. Map out your vision for the habits and goals you want to work on this year
6. Select some to work on over the coming month

7. Set out your calendar for the month
    - Plan out tasks, events, and activities that *need* to happen, schedule them in
8. Write out a list of steps you can take to work on your goals
    - Each week add some to your to-do list/planner
9. Make a monthly dashboard to hang in a prominent place to keep you motivated and on track
10. Track your habits to monitor your progress
11. Reflect on each month to see what needs adjusting and where you are progressing
12. Start again at step 6 and set your plan for the coming month.
13. Wash, rinse, repeat

"Never get so busy making a living that you forget to make a life

- Authour unknown

your wheel of life

In the wheel below, fill out your levels of contentment for each area. Each wedge is a different category. Beside each category, note your three top values for each category.

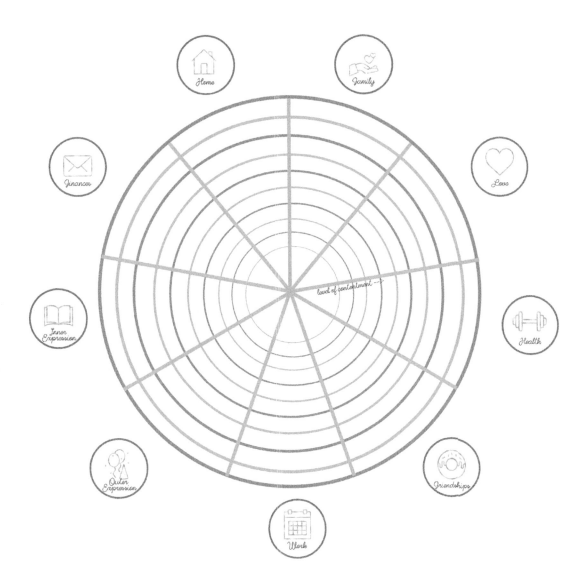

This gives you a visual of your top values and the areas of your life that need your attention.

this year's focus

Use this space to sum what you want to focus on in each category this coming year. You can do this by creating a motto, a theme word, a description of the vision, or a more of/less of table, etc. — as it pertains to each category.

lay out the whole vision

Use this space to put your whole life vision into a visual layout that appeals to you (lists, collage, word cloud, bubbles, charts, etc.). This will help you see the big picture of the vision you have for your whole life.

plan the coming year

Your whole life vision is for your WHOLE LIFE, it might not all get done in one year.

To choose where to start, focus on the areas you rated the lowest for level of contentment. Start with just one area and work up over time. This is the long game and it isn't meant to all be done at once or in one year.

Get out your calendar of choice and write down where your goals/projects can fit in. (We will cover habits after this). This means being gracious AND assertive with yourself. Consider the ways you want to push yourself while still respecting the season of life you are in.

JAN	JULY
FEB	AUG
MAR	SEPT
APR	OCT
MAY	NOV
JUNE	DEC

the goal action worksheet

Pick your first month of goals you want to work on and fill out this action sheet for each goal. This will help you identify obstacles, increase motivation and make an action plan.

Goal: Life Category:

What do I want to achieve in the next 30 days? (this needs to be specific, measurable, and actionable)

Why do I want to achieve this goal?

How will this goal improve my life? (Consider all the life categories)

How does this the idea of pursuing this goal make me feel?

What has prevented me from achieving this goal in the past?

What will this goal cost me? What will I have to give up/change?

What obstacles might get in my way this month?

What steps can I take to remove these obstacles?

What specific action steps can I take to reach this goal?

Get as detailed as you can with this. What steps need to be taken to make the next one possible? What are little steps you can take to stay motivated and moving forward? What are ways you can prepare? Every little step will help you stay the course.

If it helps you, categorize the steps you can take in ways that help you determine when and where they can be done. For example, you can categorize them by time it will take, or by the method (online, in person, from home, etc.), or the resources you will need to do it.

What resources, skills, tools will I rely on to achieve this goal?

When working on this goal is hard, what do I need to think and feel to stay motivated?

How will I know when I have achieved my goal?

How will I feel?

Powerful Habits

Changing our daily habits can have the biggest impact on our lives. Our life is the sum of our daily living.

" How we spend our days is how we spend our life"

- Annie Dillard

As Darren Hardy points out in his book *The Compound Effect,* the little things we do consistently have an exponential effect.

The most obvious example is the money you save from making your coffee at home instead of buying it everyday for $4. How about other habits — like driving instead of walking, or what you eat for breakfast, or how you talk to your family?

These little things add up in ways that we can't appreciate until we start to see their effects show up in our lives.

>> What are some current habits I have that are not positively supporting the life I want to be living?

>> What are some current habits I have that ARE positively supporting the life I want to be living?

starting small

A few years back I started an experiment called 'One Small Habit'. Each month I started a new habit that was too small to say no to. Like drinking a glass of water in the morning, or doing 10 squats while making dinner.

If changing your habits seem daunting then think of the smallest way you can start. This is called the minimum baseline. It is starting with something that you can't help but say yes to. It is one push up, or one sip of water, or one vegetable.

If you can work on growing skills in being aware of and actively trying to upgrade your habits, you will improve the quality of your life.

>> What are some big habits I want to change that I could break down into smaller ones?

habits to work on

Take the lists of habits you made in the Whole Life Vision and map out how you want to add some into your life this year.

JAN	JULY
FEB	AUG
MAR	SEPT
APR	OCT
MAY	NOV
JUNE	DEC

habit tracker

A habit tracker is a way to check off the times when you were successful in completing your new habit.

A habit tracker is a powerful tool because it makes you pay attention to yourself and your habits. In my own life, it has helped me make serious headway on changing and building habits.

Some habits I have tracked have been taking vitamins, eating vegetables, exercise, devotion, drinking water, reading. It can be anything you are working on to add as a routine in your life.

A tracker is also helpful because it allows you to see a baseline of where you are starting and work up from there. This isn't to tell you how you are failing, but instead to show you progress over time. For instance, if I have want to build a habit of eating vegetables at every meal, I won't strive for 100%. I will only ever strive for progress. I might start at 30% and give myself three months to work my way up to 90%.

Track your habits in whatever way you like: on an app, on the calendar, search online for a free 31 day tracker, use your bullet journal.

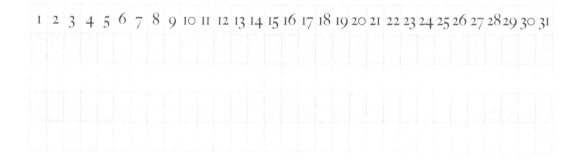

1 2 3 4 5 6 7 8 9 10 11 12 13 14 15 16 17 18 19 20 21 22 23 24 25 26 27 28 29 30 31

the habit action worksheet

Choose any habits you want to work on this month and fill out the action sheet for each one.

Habit: *Life Category:*

Why did I pick this habit?

How will it improve my life (think of all the categories)?

Describe what this habit looks like in action (when does it happen, what needs to happen, how often does it happen, etc.) This helps ensure this habit is measurable, specific and actionable.

What has prevented me from making this habit change in the past?

What might be obstacles to making this habit part of my routine?

What steps can I take to overcome these obstacles?

What do I need to give up in order to make this habit part of my life? (other habits, mindsets, resources, etc.)

What are specific actions I can take to keep accountable with making this habit part of my life?

How will I track this habit?

What will I need to remember, think and feel when I feel like quitting?

Live It Out

plan your month

1. Get out your calendar and schedule in all the 'need to do' (kid activities, events, appointments, etc.).
2. On your calendar write the goals and habits you will be focussing on this month
3. Schedule out necessary errands/appointments , etc., that are required for your goals and habits to happen this month.
4. Give a rough outline of the action steps you will take this month (this can be adjusted on a weekly basis)
5. Set up a habit tracker

plan your week

For most of us, detailed planning in weekly chunks is more realistic than for the whole month. If we take it week by week we can account for things that didn't get done last week, schedule changes, and general life happening.

Each week, take 15 minutes to plan out your week:

1. Start with a brain dump. Every task and project and idea that is in your head — put it to paper. This is a mental decluttering.
2. Prioritize from the brain dump. Highlight what needs your attention this week and add it to your calendar.
3. Write down any other 'must dos': your schedule, family schedule, the errands you need to run, the events that are happening, etc.
4. Plan out anything that makes your life easier (meals, outfits, childcare, transportation, etc.)
5. List off some 'action steps' for this month's goals that you want to fit into your week. Either schedule them now or use this list to refer as

you are available in the week (this is where the categorizing comes in handy. If you have 15 minutes, what action step could you complete in this time?)

5.   Review your habit tracker and sum up your progress for the week.

plan your day

Life on purpose shows up in the everyday operations of life. Doing the consistent, daily work of moving towards the life you want is how it actually gets done.

" Do something today that your future self will thank you for"

- Sean Patrick Flannery

Take a few minutes with your planner each morning to keep yourself on track:

1.   Review what needs to happen today and list any reminders for yourself.

2.   Plan out anything that will make your day easier.

This isn't about setting a rigid routine or to-do list, this is about reminding yourself of what you want to do. Reviewing your planner each day makes things more likely to happen.

If you have a plan for your day you will feel in control. You can see what is happening and then and you can be prepared instead of in reactive-mode

set your intentions

Setting your intention means you identify, ahead of time, how you want to show up in a given situation. This sounds strange, but it makes a whole world of difference.

To apply this to your daily life, consider what your day will look like — the places you need to go, the people you will see, the tasks you need to do. Already you can anticipate hurdles you might have, and things that might stress you out.

Instead of just rushing from one place to the next, and being reactive to the day and the people around you — you can practice being proactive with how you show up in these situations.

If you know that you will have a long drive home from school with your kids, you can set your intention on how you want to show up for that car ride. When you normally might be frustrated with traffic, or exhausted from your day you can decide to show up in the way YOU WANT. You can plan to stay calm, maybe you can do things like blast the tunes, play a game, or tell stories.

Setting your intention means you choose how you will feel and show up, on purpose. You can't decide how others will show up, or feel, or act — but you can decide for yourself.

Each day ask yourself 'What positive qualities will I bring to this day?' 'How do I want to show up?' . Then write down a simple, positive intention for your day.

Being Mindful

Like everything in life, this workbook isn't a magic solution to making your life easy and comfortable.

Vision setting, goal setting, planning, and reflecting are a vital part of the work to live your life on purpose. **The other part is the effort**, which requires a lot of attention to our mindset and thoughts.

In my experience as a life coach, this is where the most powerful and effective change happens — in our mindsets.

Part of addressing your mindset is to be MINDFUL. That means stopping and paying attention to how you are feeling and why you think you could be feeling that way.

Most of us are constantly thinking on auto-pilot. All the thoughts we have (grew up with, developed, were told to embrace) are like tracks running in our brain. Our brain is so efficient that it thinks the thoughts we have always thought without us even knowing. It is evident in our reactions to life, in the decisions we make, in how we show up for our life.

All day long we are interpreting our world and telling ourselves stories about who we are and what to expect from ourselves and others. We limit ourselves, others, and our outcomes with these mindsets and stories.

As part of this process, take the time (daily, weekly or monthly) to be mindful: How are you feeling? What story are you telling yourself? How is it affecting your results?

To practice mindfulness, set a timer throughout the day or week to stop and pause and ask yourself what is happening in your thought life. The following is a monthly reflection to help you bring mindfulness into your monthly review process.

Monthly Reflection

What worked well last month?

What didn't work well?

What felt overwhelming? *Where am I hustling for the approval of others? What system isn't working? Where is there chaos in my life that I need to address*

What habits have I been working on and how is my progress?

What goals/projects have I been working on and how is my progress?

Do any of my habits or goals need to be readjusted?

What was my biggest challenge this month?

What was my mindset around this challenge? What story did I tell myself about it? What did I make it mean?

What can I learn from this?

What mindsets will empower me in moving forward?

monthly dashboard

I recommend making yourself a one-pager for each month. This can be a vision board, a list of words, or a dashboard (like the one below).

Use this to keep motivated on what you want to be working towards this month. Post it somewhere obvious where you will see it every day (mine is in my bathroom).

PROJECTS/GOALS TO WORK ON:

HABITS TO WORK ON:

THIS MONTH I WILL . . .

Do more

Do less

Learn

Declutter

Reframe my thinking on

Be grateful for

Show love to

Accomplish

Staying on Track

accountable

Share your goals. Being accountable to someone else makes you more likely to make successful changes and reach your goals.

You might wish to hire a coach, partner with a friend, make your commitments public, or find a support group (online or offline).

Think of ways that you can be accountable to putting your Whole Life Vision into action.

motivated

As most of us experience, motivation tapers off with time. Part of doing all this work is also making a point to bring it back into focus, often.

"Whatever you focus upon, increases"

- Andy Andrews

Look for ways to keep motivated.
- Set reminders in your phone to reflect back on all this work.
- Set reminders in your phone about your vision and values.
- Subscribe to emails/podcasts/magazines that motivate you to stick to your goals.
- Set a weekly date with your accountability person
- Hire a life coach

gracious

You have spent years building up your life as it is now, it can't change in a day.

This process takes time. You will make mistakes, there will be days when you don't want to stick to it, there will be circumstances that will put a wrench in your plans. Give yourself grace. Give those around you grace.

Remember that a life on purpose isn't just the end result. It is also everything you learn on the journey to achieve it.

"It doesn't matter how slowly you go along, so long as you do not stop"

- Confucius

when you feel stuck

You will get stuck. You will want to quit. Here are some ways to get un-stuck:

- Pivot. When Plan A doesn't work, make a Plan B and try the next best thing
- Stop and be mindful. Assess what is a hurdle and how you can work around it. Focus on solutions, not the problem.
- Declutter the distractions. This might be how you are spending your time, or using your space, or your resources.
- Get help with identifying your blind spots (use the enneagram, ask a friend, work with a professional)
- If you are striving for perfect results, give yourself the gift of DONE. Done is better than perfect.

notes

the goal action worksheet

Fill out this action sheet for each goal.

Goal: *Life Category:*

What do I want to achieve in the next 30 days? (this needs to be specific, measurable, and actionable)

Why do I want to achieve this goal?

How will this goal improve my life? (Consider all the categories)

How does this the idea of pursuing this goal make me feel?

What has prevented me from achieving this goal in the past?

What will this goal cost me? What will I have to give up/change?

What obstacles might get in my way this month?

What steps can I take to remove these obstacles?

What specific action steps can I take to reach this goal?

What resources, skills, tools will I rely on to achieve this goal?

When working on this goal is hard, what do I need to think and feel to stay motivated?

How will I know when I have achieved my goal?

How will I feel?

the habit action worksheet

Choose any habits you want to work on this month and fill out the action sheet for each one.

Habit: *Life Category:*

Why did I pick this habit?

How will it improve my life (think of all the categories)?

Describe what this habit looks like in action (when does it happen, what needs to happen, how often does it happen, etc.)

What has prevented me from making this habit change in the past?

What might be obstacles to making this habit part of my routine?

What steps can I take to overcome these obstacles?

What do I need to give up in order to make this habit part of my life? (other habits, mindsets, resources, etc.)

What are specific actions I can take to keep accountable with making this habit part of my life?

How will I track this habit?

What will I need to remember, think and feel when I feel like quitting?

monthly reflection

What worked well last month?

What didn't work well?

What felt overwhelming? *Where am I hustling for the approval of others? What system isn't working? Where is there chaos in my life that I need to address*

What habits have I been working on and how is my progress?

What goals/projects have I been working on and how is my progress?

Do any of my habits or goals need to be readjusted?

What was my biggest challenge this month?

What was my mindset around this challenge? What story did I tell myself about it? What did I make it mean?

What can I learn from this?

What mindsets will empower me in moving forward?

monthly dashboard

PROJECTS/GOALS TO WORK ON:

HABITS TO WORK ON:

This month I will . . . .

Do more

Do less

Learn

Declutter

Reframe my thinking on

Be grateful for

Show love to

Accomplish

special thanks

To my husband, the love of my life, who does life on purpose right alongside me. I learn so much from you.

To my kids who inspire me to show up for my life and enjoy every single thing that is right in front of me.

To my dearest friends Sophie, Rachel and Rae, who give me life with their friendship and support.

To the readers of Simple on Purpose, who let me be part of their journey as they encourage me in my own.

to learn more

Visit me at www.simpleonpurpose.ca

Check out the Simple Saturdays email and podcast

Email me shawnascafe@gmail.com

DON'T FORGET TO LEAVE A REVIEW IN AMAZON

Made in the USA
Columbia, SC
24 March 2021

34958609R00057